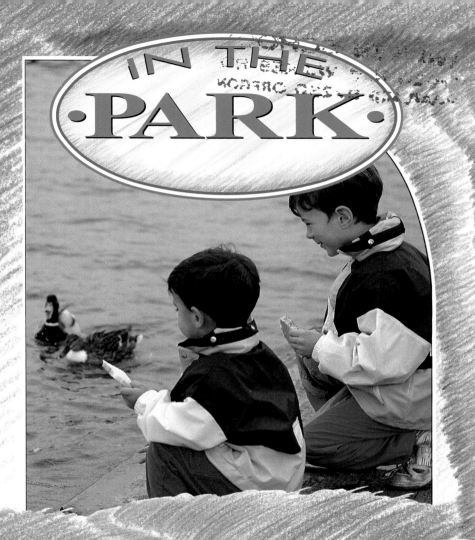

IN THE
·PARK·

In the park
I saw a bee,

and a spider's web
up in a tree.

3

A strange cocoon,
a butterfly,

and a little beetle
caught my eye.

In the park
I saw a frog,

a lizard sitting
on a log,

a mother duck,
a father drake,

and a white swan
swimming on the lake.

In the park
are many things.
Some have legs

and some have wings.

Some have spots
and lots of scales.

Some have shells
and leave long trails.

They're all alive
like you and me,

so please don't hurt
the ones you see.